Table of Contents

What Is Brand Identity?

Brand identity is the visible elements of a brand, such as color, design, and logo, that identify and distinguish the brand in consumers' minds. Brand identity is a collection of visual elements that makes your business unique and different from other businesses. Brand identity is what you, customers, and prospective customers can see and is different from brand image and branding, even though those terms are often used interchangeably. Brand identity is distinct from brand image. The former corresponds to the intent behind the branding and the way a company does the following all to cultivate a certain image in consumers' minds:

- Chooses its name
- Designs its logo

- Uses colors, shapes, and other visual elements in its products and promotions
- Crafts the language in its advertisements
- Trains employees to interact with customers

Ultimately, a brand identity is a way to communicate with the world, differentiate yourself from your competition, and create a brand experience that encourages people to engage with you. Your brand identity shapes that impression it's who you are and your values as a company. It's how you communicate your product and the catalyst that sparks the emotions you want your customers to feel each time they interact with your brand.

Understanding Brand Identity

Apple Inc. consistently tops surveys of the most effective and beloved brands because it has successfully created the impression that its products are sleek, innovative, top-of-the-line status symbols, and yet eminently useful at the same time. Apple's brand identity and brand image are closely aligned. A brand identity is made up of what your brand says, what your values are, how you communicate your product, and what you want people to feel when they interact it. Essentially, your brand identity is the personality of your business and a promise to your customers. Your personal identity consists of the things that make you stand out in a crowd. It's comprised of everything from your appearance and style to your personality and thoughts. You have a peculiar way of speaking and moving, of laughing and dressing that people associate you with. Now, look at this through the lens of marketing: You want people to recognize your brand, right off the bat a brand with an unforgettable logo, a distinct personality, and unmistakeable values. You want to have a strong brand identity Brand identity is the face of a brand. A brand is an emotional and even philosophical concept, while brand identity is the visual component of a brand that represents those larger ideas. Brand identity attracts new customers to a brand while making existing customers feel at home. It's both outward- and inward-facing.

It's vital that brand identity be consistent. Because it's representing and reinforcing the emotions of a brand, the message portrayed by brand identity components needs to be clear, and it needs to be the same no matter where it's displayed. To manage brand identity, organizations should invest in a brand management system that helps them stay consistent while still having the flexibility and the speed necessary to succeed in today's market. Components of this system might include a style guide, brand management software, and employee training.

How is Brand Identity Different from a Brand?

If brand identity is the visual part of your brand, your brand is the way people perceive and experience your firm. Think of your brand identity as an input and your brand as the output. Brand identity is not the only input, however. It works in concert with your differentiators, brand positioning, brand personality and brand messaging to influence the way the brand is perceived in the marketplace. Other influences on your brand include your customer service, online reviews, positive or negative press and how well the experience you produce matches the one you promise (your brand promise).

Jeff Bezos may have been the first to describe a brand like this: "A brand is what other people say about you when you aren't in the room." This is a useful way to think about your brand and what it will take to shape what those people say about your firm. Brand identity is one of the best tools you have to sculpt those perceptions.

KEY TAKEAWAYS

- Brand identity is the visible elements of a brand, such as color, design, and logo that identify and distinguish the brand in consumers' minds.
- Building a positive brand image can bring in consistent sales and make product roll-outs more successful.
- Building a positive, cohesive brand image requires analyzing the company and its market, and determining the company's goals, customers, and message.

Brand Identity is Crucial

John Durham, CEO of brand marketing agency Catalyst SF, stresses that brand identity is the single most important thing you can do, outside of figuring out what your business model is. Your brand identity is a necessary component to helping your business grow," and that "without it, you'll have a difficult time really building your business." Take these words to heart as you begin developing your brand identity. Soon enough, people might recognize your brand in an instant, no words or ads required.

Elements of a Strong Brand Identity

The three most valuable brands in the world Amazon, Apple, and Google are collectively worth close to $1 trillion. While most companies don't need to reach mega-brand status to stand out in their niche, there are some lessons challenger brands can take away from the giants. Most importantly, they need a solid brand strategy that will support a strong brand identity.

Brand identity isn't just a logo or an advertising campaign; it's the way a brand presents itself to the market and interacts with its audience. It covers everything from product design to audience targeting, employee relations, and customer support.

That said, just because you design those elements doesn't mean they're effective. A strong brand identity needs to work for everyone, both your internal team (e.g., brand ambassadors, content creators) and the people who will interact with it (e.g., customers). As you embark on the design process, make sure your brand identity is:

- Distinct: It stands out among competitors and catches people's attention.

- Memorable: It makes a visual impact. (Consider Apple: The logo is so memorable they only include the logo not their name on their products.)
- Scalable and flexible: It can grow and evolve with the brand.
- Cohesive: Each piece complements the brand identity.
- Easy to apply: It's intuitive and clear for designers to use.

If any of these elements are missing, it will be challenging for your brand team to do their job well. There's no aspect of a company that's not a part of its brand identity.

elements that you should address to create a strong brand identity, from the most basic to the more complex.

Name

"What's in a name?" Shakespeare famously asked. When it comes to branding, the answer is "a lot." A name identifies, differentiates, and reflects the essence of the owner, and the same is true for brands. The brand name is the company's first impression; it's strengthened by good customer experiences and destroyed by bad ones. Choosing a name isn't a straightforward process, so it helps to follow a few basic principles to make sure the name advances the overall brand strategy:

- Be simple. While sophisticated wordplay might be tempting, it's more important to be understood. A good brand name is easy to pronounce and conveys the brand's purpose and character. When part of a broad, rich brand strategy, even the simplest names are the most powerful. Think Apple, Facebook, or Toys "R" Us.

- Be memorable. The strongest memories are emotion-based, and powerful brand names do an excellent job of conveying emotion. For example, Land Rover taps into a sense of adventure and escape.

- Be original. A strong brand name must be one of a kind, and that's a tough ask in a saturated global marketplace. Yet, there are many ways to convey originality. Did you know that the brand name IKEA is an acronym of the founder's name and hometown? Or that the name Lego is an abbreviation of two Danish words meaning "play well"? A genuinely unique name has another advantage it'll be easier to obtain trademarks, and domain names are more likely to be available.

Audience

Part of building a strong brand identity is boosting brand awareness and perception, and this can only be done correctly by targeting the right audience. For example, if the target audience is new mothers, a brand will naturally focus its advertising strategy on parenting websites and online wellness forums. If the audience is teenagers, it might include native ads on gaming sites or sports channels. According to the Content Marketing Institute, 90% of top-performing B2B content marketers focus on what information the audience needs, rather than what the brand wants to say.

Having a deep understanding of who your audience is, what matters to them, and what their needs and challenges are should directly shape a company's brand from the visual design to the development of a brand's core values. Everything should center around the target audience.

Logo

Neuroscientific research at MIT demonstrated that the brain could process images in 13 milliseconds, and logos provide instant brand recognition. The world's most famous brands are recognizable by their logo alone, which is why companies place so much importance (and so many resources) in logo development. BP spent millions of pounds introducing its new sunflower logo to the market, and it was still met with controversy.

A brand logo should be instantly recognizable: simple, unique, appropriate, and memorable. Most importantly, it should clearly convey the company's messaging. Companies should also consider the various sizes and shapes their logo will be expected to take, from website headers to products to stationary. Make sure the logo either scales easily or comes in variations that fit common shapes and media.

Look and Feel

Strong brand identity comes from high design standards applied consistently in every aspect of the brand's strategy from office design to product packaging, web design, and social media posts. This is achieved with a brand style guide or brand book. A solid brand book consists of a wide range of information governing the brand's precise look and feel: font types and sizes, brand colors, logo design and size, layout rules, and more. Small discrepancies in design can erode brand identity, even seemingly trivial matters such as letter spacing of the brand name can have a negative effect. A brand book can help prevent that from happening.

Unique Value Proposition

A critical element of any brand strategy is defining the brand's unique value proposition (UVP). The UVP describes how the brand is different from its competitors, its benefit to customers, and how it solves their pain points. By clearly outlining the brand's value offering, the UVP also establishes the brand's positioning in the market. A UVP doesn't need to be complex or sophisticated, but it should be clear and descriptive. Take the UVP of raw cookie dough maker, DŌ: "the original gourmet edible and bakeable cookie dough confectionery." It clearly describes the product ("cookie dough confectionary"), its features ("edible and bakeable"), while positioning the brand as "the original" and "gourmet" in relation to competitors.

Thought Leadership

An effective way to strengthen brand identity is by cultivating a market position as a thought leader. Thought leadership is when an individual or company is recognized as an authority in its field or niche. It's a cost-efficient way to build a brand presence as it harnesses the inherent skill, talent, and charisma of the company's team. Thought leaders are sought out for their expertise and opinions and often feature in articles, blog posts, industry journals, webinars, podcasts, live speaking events, TV, and more. Imagine Microsoft without Bill Gates or Tesla without Elon Musk. The good news for smaller businesses is that thought leaders don't have to be world-famous to have a significant impact on brand strategy.

Brand Values

Every memorable brand stands for something, whether it's something global like saving the environment or something specific like making clothes that fit every body shape. These brand values help the company focus its efforts towards a set of unified goals, often expressed as aspirational statements or promises. They also help to cement a brand in the minds of its target audience, giving them a powerful bonding tool with the people they hope to market to.

Failing to create and communicate brand values leads to brands that don't really feel "alive" brands that remain abstract and corporate, and don't resonate with any audience. Some executives see this as a positive: If you don't align yourself with any specific values, you won't risk accidentally turning off any potential customers. Unfortunately, these companies also won't attract any prospective customers and run the risk of creating a brand that doesn't stand out from competitors.

Setting and communicating brand values is essential to creating a lasting brand image. The values a company picks should reflect the values of its audience and staff they also have to be reflected in their marketing and their products. Most of all, any brand values a company espouses need to be held as sacred and unbreakable. Customers might shop with an organization that doesn't have clear values, but they won't shop with one that breaks their brand promises.

Memorability

Over three-quarters of consumers make purchasing decisions because of the brand. That's why it's so important to cultivate brand memorability. It's tempting to think that memorable brands are the ones appearing in Super Bowl ads or flashing on billboards in Times Square. That may be true of the world's largest and most famous brands, but any brand can achieve memorability without spending millions of advertising dollars to do it. Brand memorability comes from some of the most basic strategies, such as excellent customer service and responsiveness, high product quality, and authentic marketing messages. Take the below Christmas video, produced for $130 by a mom-and-pop hardware store in Wales, UK. They didn't need an advertising agency or six-figure budget to create a powerful, memorable campaign that got over 2 million YouTube views in 2 weeks.

Employee Advocacy

More and more brands realize the power of their employees in building a strong brand identity. Some of the statistics surrounding employee advocacy are truly impressive brand messages shared by employees got 561% higher reach than those promoted by regular brand channels. Plus, employee advocacy contributed to a 65% increase in brand recognition. Employees of an organization are natural partners in brand marketing; they know the company inside out, and they have a personal stake in the brand's success. In the best case, they're loyal and proud of the brand, creating a positive flow of brand messaging to their social and personal networks. Employee advocacy is also prized for its high ROI brands can boost their reach and exposure at minimal cost, simply by providing content for employees to share.

Cohesion

A strong brand identity is a coherent one. It provides a consistent, logical, and satisfying customer experience that fulfills the promise of the company's unique value proposition. Of course, a key aspect of brand cohesion is making sure there's consistency in design across all marketing activities, such as websites, social media pages, and ad campaigns. However, true brand cohesion is much more than that. It means not just fulfilling customers' current needs and expectations, but anticipating new ones as they arise, and before the customers even realize they have them. Brand cohesion demands a flexible, integrated organizational infrastructure that supports this dynamic approach.

Brand identity is a broad concept, and it can be challenging to know where to begin. With the help of the elements outlined above, brands large and small can build an identity that engages and excites their target audience while remaining true to their authentic values. That's the basis for an effective brand strategy

What Does a Brand Identity Include?

A logo and a color palette alone do not make a brand identity. When designing your identity, you need to create a comprehensive visual language that can be applied to everything from your website to your packaging. Depending on your brand (and the type of content you plan to create), your needs may be more expansive, but a basic brand identity includes:

- Logo
- Colors
- Typography
- Design System
- Photography
- Illustration
- Iconography
- Data visualization

- Interactive elements
- Video and motion
- Web design

Your brand identity should translate across mediums, so include everything you need to make sure it does.

Logo

A brand identity is an intricate design system. Each element influences the other, but it starts with your logo.

Colors

Once you have a solid logo, you can explore your color palette. Color is a great tool to differentiate your brand from competitors, but know that color can also elicit strong emotions, so choose wisely.

Typography

Every visual element in your identity should contribute to a cohesive visual language, and thus each should complement the other. This is particularly true of typography, which should be informed by the shape of your logo.

Design System

This is often a weak point in visual languages. Brands think that because they have their logo, color, and typography set, they can combine them however they like. But because brand identity is all about introducing yourself to people effectively, it's important to make it an enjoyable experience. In information design, that means providing a truly consistent and cohesive presentation.

Photography

Photography plays a huge role in your brand identity, from your product images to your advertising. It's important to identify clear guidelines about the types of images (and visual treatments) that are and aren't appropriate.

Illustration

When it comes to illustration, you need a cohesive and uniform language. Don't over-illustrate or use clashing styles. Instead, think of how your illustration will be used in conjunction with other visual elements.

Iconography

Good iconography is influenced not just by the creative visual language but by the applications for the work. It depends on what your product or service is, as well as the industry and medium (e.g., web-only vs. UI vs. sales brochures).

Data Visualization

Data should be designed for clarity and comprehension, in addition to aesthetic appeal. Thus, it's important to design visualizations that adhere to data visualization best practices.

Why is brand identity so important?

As the embodiment of almost everything your business is and does, according to Purely Branded, a brand "lives and evolves in the minds and hearts" of consumers. Its identity, therefore, is crucial to the business's future.

So, if your brand is more than just its logo, how can you replicate what brands like Coca-Cola have done and tap these other elements of your business's identity? Here are six components of a well-developed brand identity, and why it's so important for you to develop them.

The "Face" of Your Business

For all intents and purposes, your brand's logo is the "face" of your business. But that face should do more than just look cool or interesting a logo's contribution to brand identity is associative, too. It tells the public that [this image] means [the name of your company].

Credibility and Trust

Having a brand identity doesn't just make your product more memorable; it makes your brand more authoritative in the marketplace. A brand that establishes a face, and maintains that face consistently over time, develops credibility among its competitors and trust among its customers.

Advertising Impressions

A brand identity is a template for everything you would include on an advertisement for your business whether that ad is in print, online, or a preroll commercial on YouTube. A brand with a face and industry credibility is well prepared to promote itself and make impressions on potential buyers.

Your Company's Mission

When you create an identity for your brand, you're giving it something to stand for. That, in turn, gives your company a purpose. We all know companies have mission statements, right? Well, you can't have one without first giving your brand an identity.

Generating New Customers and Delighting Existing Ones

A brand identity one with a face, trust, and a mission attracts people who agree with what your brand has to offer. But once these people become customers, that same brand identity gives them a sense of belonging. A good product generates customers, but a good brand generates advocates.

If you want your business to become a well-known and beloved brand name, it's going to take some work. The following steps will help you build a brand identity. They are simple steps; implementing them, however, is another story.

Strong Brand Identity Examples

- Coca-Cola
- Hustle & Hope Greeting Cards
- POP Fit
- Burt's Bees
- Asana
- Semicolon Bookstore & Gallery

1. Coca-Cola

When you hear the name Coca-Cola, you probably picture its well-known logo,

But you also might think of the polar bear, the color red, its "Share a Coke" campaign, or the classic ribbon-like imagery featured on its cans. Here are two things that comprise Coca-Cola's brand identity:

- Coca-Cola's brand identity begins with a red logo in script text. The red color elicits confidence in the person who drinks a Coke, while the script typeface is all about enjoyment. Coffee, for example, is a drink you have before work in the morning. Coca-Cola is a drink you enjoy when you're done in the afternoon. This is the brand's "face."

- Coca-Cola prints its logo on a uniquely shaped bottle (it's true, no other beverages have bottles exactly like it). This tells customers they're not getting an imitation this is the real thing. The brand develops credibility and trust this way.

2. **Hustle & Hope Greeting Cards**

 Hustle & Hope is a brand that positions their products as more than a greeting card. Their stationary and cards tackle more difficult topics such as job hunting and personal development. By pairing simple inspirational messaging with a code on the back of the card that leads to digital content and tips, the cards are meant to "level up" the recipient in some way.

Founder Ashley Sutton always wanted to start a stationery company, but after a career working in some of the top Fortune 500 companies, she became passionate about empowering people to be their best professional selves. That's when she had an epiphany that would later become the basis of what makes her company unique: "Why not sell cool greeting cards AND help people!" Here's how this brand's identity is executed:

- All the paper products use modern, colorful designs that pop off the page and slogans that go beyond generic well wishing.
- The experience of scanning the code is a novelty that makes an impression, both with the product itself as well as its mission to drive an idea home.

3. POP Fit

POP Fit has a beautiful brand with bright pinks, purples, and yellows, but that's not even a main element of their brand identity. Perhaps one of the most stunning thing about this brand is their radical representation found in all their messaging. According to their website, "POP Fit Clothing was built on the idea that representation, inclusivity, and body positivity matters in both fashion and media." This is why their sizes range from XXS to 4XL and feature signature fabric with a four-way stretch.

- POP Fit's advertising supports their message of inclusivity, featuring women of color, wheelchair users, and diverse body types. Their images are also unretouched, showcasing their diverse models realistically and respectfully.
- Their products solve for massive pains in the athletic clothing industry, such as sizing issues, lack of pockets, and

transparency or rolling while doing squats and other exercises.

4. **Burt's Bees**

After humble beginnings in beekeeping and selling honey, Burt's Bees grew to meet the need for all-natural and sustainable personal products. The company seeks to "make thoughtful choices to reduce our impact on nature and work to protect biodiversity, which preserves our own place in the world."

Their initial logo (pictured above) depicting the bearded founder underscores the feeling of simplicity and modesty. This is in stark contrast to aesthetics that other beauty and personal care products embody.

Here's how else the brand distances itself from flashiness, sticking to its nature-obsessed focus:

- Burt's Bees responsibly sources ingredients for their products and use recyclable packaging.
- They give to conservation projects and other green initiatives.

5. Asana

Asana's mission is "to help humanity thrive by enabling the world's teams to work together effortlessly." The founders began at Facebook, where it was clear that they needed a project management and collaboration tool, and it was clear that their creation impacted the company in a positive way.

In Sanskrit, "Asana" refers to a specific pose in which yogis sit, and the company name is in homage to the Buddhist principles of focus and flow. This along with their values of "doing great things, fast" and teamwork is manifested clearly in their visual brand as well:

- Asana uses a lot of white space for focus with bursts of color to "inject energy" into the workspace.
- The three dots in the logo are arranged together, signifying balance and collaboration.

6. **Semicolon Bookstore & Gallery**

Semicolon Books was born when owner/operator Danielle Mullen chose to seize the day. After being diagnosed with a tumor on her ocular nerve, she was thinking about legacy. Then, without expectation or intention to open a store, she walked by the perfect space for lease. Not long after, the spot was hers, and she was building shelves.

The book store's mission is in "nurturing the connection between literature, art, and the pursuit of knowledge; while also using the power of words to better our community." Because of this, the brand is committed to the Chicago community and cultivating a welcoming space for their customers:

- Their #ClearTheShelves initiative allows local students to take home any books they want, free of charge, to impact literacy rates in Chicago.

- Residents are encouraged to BYOB, chill in the store, and talk with the owner, creating an air of friendliness and camaraderie.

- Semicolon Bookstore supports local creators from featuring local artists in the gallery and showcasing local authors.

- You'll also notice that their visual brand calls out the Chicago vibe while showing people reading and enjoying the store.

- In the above examples, brand is so much bigger than the logo or visuals for the business.

-

How to Create a Brand Identity

- Research your audience, value proposition, and competition.
- Design the logo and a template for it.
- Integrate language you can use to connect, advertise, and embody on social media.
- Know what to avoid.
- Monitor your brand to maintain its brand identity.

1. Research your audience, value proposition, and competition.

Just like any other aspect of starting a business, the first step in creating a brand identity is to complete market research. You should clarify and understand these five things.

Audience

It's no secret that different people want different things. You can't (usually) target a product to a pre-teen the same way you would target a product to a college student. Learning what your audience wants from a business in your industry is vital to creating a brand people will love.

Value Proposition & Competition

What makes your business unique in your industry? What can you offer your consumers that others can't? Knowing the difference between you and your competition is imperative to developing a successful brand. Keeping an eye on your competitors will also educate you on what branding techniques work well and those that don't.

Mission

You know what your business offers, but be sure to have a clear and direct mission statement that describes your vision and goals. In other words, know your business's purpose you can't very well create a personality for a business unless you know what that business is about.

Personality

Even though you're not necessarily branding an individual, that doesn't mean that you can't be personable when developing a brand image. Use your type, colors, and imagery to represent who the brand is. Then enhance that visual representation with your tone of voice: Are you a confident business with a lot of sass, like Nike? Or are you ritzy and professional, like Givenchy? Either way, be sure to develop your brand as a way to represent your business.

Research may be boring, but the more you know about your business, the stronger your brand identity will be.

SWOT Analysis

Finally, completing a SWOT Analysis can be beneficial to better understand your brand. Considering the characteristics of the brand will help you find characteristics you want to portray in the brand. SWOT stands for:

- Strengths: Positive characteristics of your business that provide an advantage over your competition.

- Weaknesses: Characteristics that prove to be a disadvantage to your business.

- Opportunities: Changes and trends in your industry that offer opportunities for your business.

- Threats: Elements in the environment or industry that may cause problems for your business.

2. **Design the logo and a template for it.**

Once you know your business inside and out, it's time to bring your brand to life. In the words of graphic designer Paul Rand, "Design is the silent ambassador of your brand." Here's what you'll need to know:

Logo

Although the logo is not the entirety of the brand identity, it's a vital element in the branding process it's the most recognizable part of your brand. It's on everything from your website to your business cards to your online ads. With your logo on all of these elements, your branding should look as cohesive as this example:

Interesting Form

As imperative as your logo is to branding, it's not the only element that makes a brand identity strong. Your product(s), the packaging, or the way you present your services all need to play a part in your brand identity. Visually representing your business in everything you do will create consistency and help create a familiarity with your consumers. Take McDonald's golden arches for example. They used an interesting form to create the iconic "M," which is now recognizable all over the world.

Color & Type

Creating a color palette is a way to enhance your identity. It provides you with variety so you can create unique designs for your business while remaining faithful to the brand identity.

Type can also be a double-edged sword if not utilized properly. Although "mix and match" type design has become quite the trend, that doesn't mean mixing a handful of fonts is necessarily a good idea for your business. In your logo, on your website, and on any documents that your business creates (print and digital), there should be consistent use of typography. If you take a look at Nike's website and its ads, it keeps the same typeface and type style throughout all aspects of the business and it works wonders for them.

Templates

You probably send out emails, type up letters, or hand out business cards to potential customers on a daily basis. Creating templates (even for a detail as minute as email signatures) will give your business a more unified, credible, and professional look and feel.

Consistency

As mentioned in nearly every step already (I can't stress it enough), consistency is what can make or break a brand identity. Use the aforementioned templates and follow the design choices you've decided upon for your brand throughout all areas of your business to create a harmonious brand identity.

Flexibility

Yes, consistency is crucial but remaining flexible in a society that is always looking for the next best thing is just as important. Flexibility allows for adjustments in ad campaigns, taglines, and even some modernizing to your overall brand identity so you can continuously keep your audience interested. The key is keeping any changes you make consistent throughout your entire brand (e.g., don't change the design of your business cards and nothing else).

Document

One of the most effective ways to ensure a business sticks to its branding "rules" is to create a set of brand guidelines that document all of the do's and don'ts of your brand. Skype is one brand that has done an amazing job creating a clear, cohesive brand guide that anyone can follow. This is one way to empower people to build brand assets and share your brand while remaining brand compliant.

Integrate language you can use to connect, advertise, and embody on social media.

Now that you've established your brand within your company and have taken all the necessary steps to develop it, you're ready to integrate your brand within your community.

And one of the most successful ways to accomplish this is for your brand to provide quality content. In HubSpot's ebook Branding in the Inbound Age, Patrick Shea writes, "In every way, your content is your brand online. It's your salesperson, your store, your marketing department; it's your story, and every piece of content you publish reflects on, and defines, your brand. So, great content, great brand. Boring content, boring brand."

Language

Use language that matches that personality of your brand. If your brand identity is high-end, use professional language; if your brand is laid-back, be more conversational. The language you choose to use as a brand will be integrated throughout the entire business, so it's important that you carefully craft your tone to match your brand's personality.

Connection & Emotion

People love stories. More accurately, people love stories that move them (emotionally and to action). A strong brand identity can establish an emotional connection with consumers, which can be a solid foundation for building a lasting relationship with a brand.

Advertise

Designing ads, whether traditional or digital, is the most efficient way of introducing your brand to the world. It's a way to get the message of your brand seen and heard by your target audience.

Social Media

Another great way to establish a connection with your consumers is through social media. The plethora of platforms on the internet offers up a ton of digital real estate you can use to establish your brand identity. Coca-Cola, once again, makes great use of its Facebook cover photo real estate by keeping it consistent with the happiness theme.

Social media is also important when it comes to conversing directly with your customers and creating affinity for your brand. If you're mentioned in a tweet, status, or post (especially if the customer has a question or concern), be sure to give your brand a good reputation by responding efficiently to your customers.

4. **Know what to avoid.**

You can follow all the steps of creating a strong brand identity, but if you're guilty of any of the following practices, your brand might falter or fail.

Don't give your customers mixed messages.

Know what you want to say, and use the appropriate language and visuals to say it. Just because it makes sense to you doesn't mean it will make sense to your customers.

Don't copy your competitors.

Your competition may have exemplary branding, and since you're selling the same products or services, you might want to do what you know works don't. Take what they do into account, and put your own twist on it to make your business stand out in your industry even more.

Don't lose consistency between online and offline

Yes, your print material might look a little different than your online presence, but your colors, type, theme, and message should all be consistent.

5. Monitor your brand to maintain its brand identity.

Similar to other aspects of your marketing, it's difficult to know what you're doing right (and what you're not) without tracking key performance metrics. Use Google Analytics, surveys, comments, social media discussions, etc., to monitor your brand and get a sense of how people talk about and interact with you. This will give you the opportunity to implement changes to your brand as needed, whether it's to correct a mistake or to improve brand identity.

Creating a memorable brand requires consistent use of type, color, images, and language, but it's worth it. When consumers instantly recognize who you are and what you stand for all based on a logo, you've become more than just a name and a symbol.

 Building a brand identity is a multi-disciplinary strategic effort, and every element needs to support the overall message and business goals. It can include a company's name, logo, and design; its style and the tone of its copy; the look and composition of its products; and, of course, its social media presence. Apple founder Steve Jobs famously obsessed over details as small as the shade of gray on bathroom signs in Apple stores. While that level of focus may not be necessary, the anecdote shows that Apple's successful branding is the result of intense effort, not

serendipity.